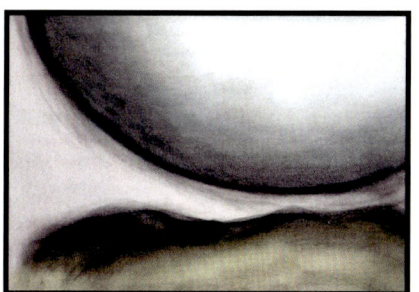

Drawing into Creative Wholeness

meditation and visual expression as a spiritual practice

Cameron Sesto

a cameronart book

Dedicated to the past, present, and future seekers of creative wholeness.

" . . .the seed of the new is present in the shell of the old. Trust your own process."
~ Book of Runes

© 2014 Cameron Sesto
Text, Illustrations, Design and Production.
Available on Amazon.com

"You can only expect a fulfilling life if you dedicate yourself to finding out who you are, to finding the ineffable, idiosyncratic seeds of possibility already planted inside. There is some surrender required here."

-Stephen Cope, The Great Work of your Life.

Introduction

There is a dimension of great depth within you—a place where intuition resides.
Your intuition knows before anything is explained using words.
You can access this place of knowing, this place of spirit in many ways.
Mickey Hart talks about it in terms of his music. His drumming brings him into spirit.
Lauren Artress teaches us about walking the labyrinth—releasing cares as we walk toward the center. Revelation and insight occurring once we arrive at the center, then walking along the paths of the labyrinth back to where we began, refreshed and renewed; returning to the familiar with new awareness. Gabrielle Roth talked about her dancing. She described her physical movements in the form of five rhythms that she considers our body's native language: flowing, staccato, chaos, lyrical, and stillness; *act them out, enter into them,* she says.

It is difficult to go from the full-speed-ahead of the everyday to being a witness to one's interior meandering. That's why it is helpful to have a "practice" in place. A time of the day or a time of the week when you can enter a sacred place with the intention of delving deep, allowing impressions to flow from the subconscious to the conscious mind. I enter the realm of my spirit through a meditative silence in the evening — once a week with my workshop participants. It is within the silence I gather images that are meaningful to me. Then immediately afterward, by the light of just one candle, I draw — draw down an image, the feelings, the impressions, in abstract lines or tones, or write the words that come to me during the meditation. I use big wide arm movements on large pads of paper, letting go into the silence with *feeling charged* strokes of black charcoal—quietly flowing, lyrical or still, making whisper light grey strokes or dark loud chaotic or staccato black marks on the white paper. I blur the charcoal marks with the back of my hand or lightly smudge them with the trace of a single fingertip. Sometimes I make three or four drawings, other times six or seven. I experience a present-tense freedom from critical, judgmental thoughts about my drawing ability. When the lights are turned on, these drawings provide me with visual evidence/symbols of my inner thoughts.

A visual exploration of the Self created by drawing with charcoal after meditating is a passionate response to a non-verbal communication with the Self.

Each week for more than 25 years, I have meditated with others and drawn down my inner experience with charcoal on paper. We affectionately call this work: MedArt. Nothing about this process has become repetitious or boring. Rather, this has become a rudder to my week, a place of centering where I come back into balance and can respond rather than react to what comes into my life during the week. I have gained self-knowledge from a place of experiencing the deep waters of my being rather than believing only what appears reflected on the outer surface of my daily life. With continued practice, I went deeper into the meditations, my understanding broadened, and when I better understood myself, I better understood others. I had more to give and could open myself to receiving more from others.

This book will introduce you to my workshop, *Drawing into Creative Wholeness,* and the process of combining meditation with visual expression that I have found to be very successful with my own work as an artist and a spiritual seeker. Since 1986, I have met weekly with a small group to meditate and draw. I notice that when a participant reaches a new level of self-confidence, they will leave the

Newburyport Daily News, Thursday, February 27, 1986 B1

Artists offer course on gaining inspiration through meditation

NEWBURYPORT — A new course using meditation as a source of inspiration for art called "Drawing From The Well" is being offered here by Judy Platz and Cameron Sesto at the Pressroom Gallery on Merrimac Street.

" 'Drawing From The Well' is an idea which grew from pursuing a method to help the visual artist tap his/her subconscious sources and then bring back those images as translations onto paper," Platz said.

"As Carl Jung wrote about it, we carry with us in our subconscious ancient images around which we build our lives and which are limitless sources of inspiration, growth and healing," she continued.

"What this course offers is the meditative structure for the artist to become more familiar with individualistic depths so when he/she approaches the canvas or paper, the intellect is working as one with the emotion behind the stroke."

Cameron Sesto is an artist. She and her husband, Carl Sesto, have worked in many different forms of the visual arts over the past 20 years.

Currently, they create and sell fine art original lithographs in their studio, The Pressroom Gallery. Cameron Sesto's art jewelry was profiled recently in "North Shore Life Magazine."

Judy Platz teaches meditation and healing classes, bringing to this work many years of experience as a social worker. She also is a journalist and poet.

"Drawing From The Well" classes will be held at The Pressroom Gallery on Tuesday evenings late in March. The fee will be $10 per each two-hour class for five weeks. Students should bring newsprint pad and charcoal stick. For further information, call Cameron Sesto at The Pressroom Gallery,

KEITH SULLIVAN PHOTO

Cameron Sesto and Judy Platz doing free association drawings which represent images brought up out of the unconscious after meditation.

group and a new person appears who wants to join us. The flow is organic. Those who benefit the most stay for three years or more and leave having formed new relationships, new careers (rather than jobs), or new jobs that provide greater satisfaction and respect. Participating weekly with a relatively consistent group of people heals the spirit by focusing on deep positive communion with others rather than chatting about the negative influences that we find surrounding us from the daily news to the latest problem for ourselves or others.

My workshop offers a meditative structure that enables students to become more familiar with their individual depths while sharing this experience with others. When you put charcoal to paper using only your hands, the intellect and emotions work as one to create the stroke. The charcoal sketches I've made during these weekly meetings have provided me with an abundance of creative imagery that goes beyond what I think, and touches the *who I am* core of my being. I can stand back and exclaim: *"Look what came through me!"* Instead of: *"Look what I did!"*

I am grateful for the gifts each image provides and grateful for those who share this journey with me.

There are five main steps to our exploration:

Connection: What is it about reading a course in a catalog that makes you say: *"Yes."* Desire, curiosity, or perhaps a feeling an inner connection that pulls you toward trying a workshop, joining a group or committing to a practice.

Meditating: Meditating within a group and being willing to put oneself in a place of receptivity puts us in a position of vulnerability. There is a need to surrender to what comes to us and a surrender to a willingness to share with the others in our group.

Finding Voice: We find our unique visual voice by learning how to use the medium of charcoal with just our hands and fingers. We can create extra dark lines and tones as well as the very lightest grays using our whole hand or just a finger or two.

Sharing: We allow others to see our visual voice and comment on our stories. We also listen to the journey others have taken and give them our positive feedback.

Manifesting and Integration: By bringing greater awareness and self-confidence to our every day lives, we begin to trust our intuition; where to best put our energies, and where we need the courage to change when change is demanded. When we do bring forth our true creative selves, we will manifest and live a life of creative wholeness.

Release ~1999

Meditation

"What lies behind us and what lies before us are tiny matters compared to what lies within us."

Ralph Waldo Emerson

At first I was afraid of the quiet.
Wasn't it dark in that silent void? Would I drift off into night echo's and not return?

In 1985, my fears were as numerous as my excuses for not learning to meditate in spite of many people, who for years, encouraged me to try it. Then my friend Judith Platz, living right down the street, suggested I attend her six week introduction to meditation course free of charge.
No more excuses, I had to say yes.

Instead of being caught in a frightening, silent darkness, I entered a sun drenched visual cornucopia containing everything from the mundane to the profound. I had lifted the corner of a heavy red velvet curtain and for a few moments each week, caught a glimpse of life behind the *stage*. What I didn't realize then was that, little by little, I was revealing the invisible, deeper side of my life. I loved it! This led to my asking: "What if I could draw right after meditating, before we started talking?" So I invited three friends to join me in my studio to try it out. The result was the creation of my *Drawing into Wholeness Workshop* meeting once a week in the evening for two to two and a half hours.

This workshop does not offer a linear process of learning something specific, but rather aims to bring together people who are interested in exploring their creative inner selves. If you asked each person who joined with me for this process of inner exploration, each of them would probably give a different reason for signing up.

There were five of us wanting to explore this process back in 1986: an artist, a graphic designer, a photographer, a potter and myself. We came together for the purpose of sharing a meditation and an art experience. However, there were many other issues we each brought to our meetings. Even if we weren't aware of it, there were parts of each of us demanding change. And change we did. As I see it now, it's a bit like looking at faint stars—in order to see them clearly we have to look slightly to the left or right of the star. The same thing happens when individuals come together with a variety of wounds. When we don't speak of the wounds, but speak rather of our artwork, its spiritual content, and offer praise and encouragement to one another once a week, the healing begins.

A caring wind blew among us. Each of us felt the unspoken support. By the time this particular group of participants disbanded after meeting once a week for almost five years, every one of us had made changes in our lives. Each of us began saying "yes" to a part of ourselves that was truly meaningful. When we meet with others once a week and receive unconditional support, we receive the gift of self-knowledge which then leads to greater self-confidence, intuitive understanding, compassion for others, and courage to take the actions necessary for change.

The artist, from the wound of addictive behaviors, pulled herself free, let go of her distrust of people and entered a successful personal relationship. Both her business and personal life bloomed. The graphic designer who was working under an abusive boss, changed jobs and was delighted with the new supervisor's support and much higher pay. The potter who was working cleaning people's homes—with many back problems, opened her own studio and began a successful teaching career.

How did this all happen?

It sounds so simple: just make a few quick changes and life is on a new track. However, changing one's life by letting go of familiar behaviors is difficult. The ruts have been made deep by days, months, and years of repetition. However, when one thing changes for the positive, it will change everything without trying, without effort, without "pushing the river."

There is a difference between what is *seen* within the meditative state and *daydreaming* or *thinking*. What is important is to allow oneself to be in a state of receptivity. Being more aware than usual there is more attention placed on what is seen. Sometimes the flow of perception or imagination may result in a flash of aesthetic insight or creative inspiration. Our drawing after meditating subconsciously reinforces what we learn . Week after week, strength, courage, and intuition grow. Making life changes becomes natural. Inner growth demands a reflection of that growth in the outer world.

The Studio where we work is dimly lit. Only one candle burns on a tall candlestick on the floor next to my Buddha. We each select a cotton mat to sit on and put our cushions and our large (18 x 24 inch) drawing pad on the floor near us. There's plenty of room for everyone to feel safe and private.

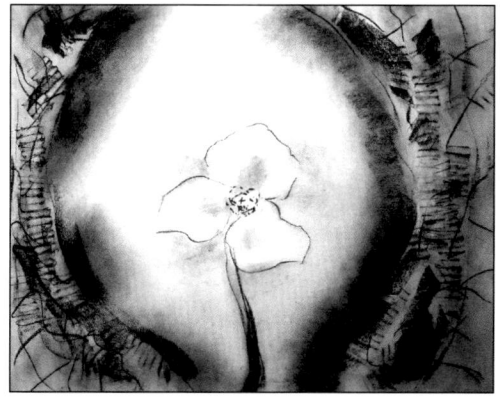

Sanctuary~2014

I wrote a guided meditation back in 1986 and have now put it on a CD. We play this, or one of several different meditations that will bring us into the meditative space, silence for twenty minutes, and then return us in a gentle way. One CD we listen to often is a simple ringing of a Tibetan bowl at the beginning and at the end of the meditation.

The CD is important so I can join the group as one of the participants. There is no one teacher, no authority other than what can be found within each of us. As the facilitator, I offer the space and the structure. We all begin together, end meditating together, but finish our drawings at different times.

My aim during the meditation time is to quiet my mind and allow images and thoughts to present themselves without judgment. Dropping down into the meditation my breathing slows my brain waves— gently sliding from Beta, through Alpha into Theta rhythms. The silence offers up images and ideas allowing me to leave my daily life behind for awhile and explore my inner landscape.

Some thoughts or images arise that I don't give any attention to and let them pass by; others I will focus on and take a deeper look. I allow myself to be in a state of receptivity so I can perceive what's going on. The meditation is a place where the imagery takes precedence over language. Sometimes, it's only after the drawing that the words take form and I understand what I've seen. I learned years later that Carl Jung called this type of meditation *active imagination.*

Robert Johnson details this process in his book: **Inner Work**—*using dreams and active imagination for personal growth.* The idea that images are symbols we can learn from has been spoken about by many of my favorite authors such as: Joseph Campbell in his *Power of Myth*, Bernie Siegal in *How to Live between Office Visits,* James W. Jones *In the Middle of This Road We Call Our Life,* and the Gospel of Philip as quoted by Elaine Pagels in her book: *The Gnostic Gospels.*

Sometimes what flows in and out of the meditation seems so boring, other times mundane, and then there are those moments when what I've seen or intuited has been a revelation. When I observe my thoughts over long periods of time, I gain a better understanding of my own cycles of creativity and growth. Spending time to develop, experience, learn and return to the beginning again and again is an unusual pursuit. But for this process to function at it's best, time is very much needed.

This reminds me of one of my favorite quotes from Joseph Campbell when being interviewed by Bill Moyers in **The Power Of Myth**:

Moyers: "What does it mean to have a sacred place?"

Campbell: " . . . This is a place where you can simply experience and bring forth what you are and what you may be. This is the place of creative incubation. At first you may find that nothing happens there. But if you have a sacred place and use it, something eventually will happen."

And this wonderful quote by Hilary Hart in **Body of Wisdom**:

"Spiritual transformation seems to always depend on creative space, on knowing when and how to watch and protect space for transpersonal and divine energies to emerge. In individual practice, meditation and prayer are containers for just this kind of process. Both require a time and space to turn inward, away from outer distractions of the day and inner distractions of mental chatter. They open our being to what flows from the inner worlds."

The Blessing Bowl ~2001

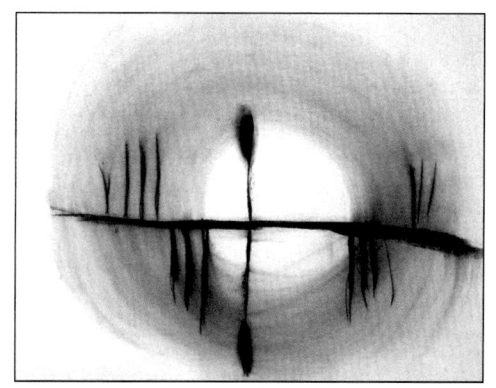

Finding Voice: Drawing with Charcoal

My intention is to become familiar with my unique visual expression.
My visual voice in charcoal becomes familiar by doing the work.
By doing the work I become familiar with the process.
When I become familiar with the process,
I can trust the process.
I can then lean into doing the work without the burden of expected results.

There is no direct access to truth just as there is no direct access to happiness or success. These qualities cannot be pursued but must ensue. Paying attention is key. What I *can* do is direct my attention, focus, and then do the work. I won't judge the results but rather commit to the process. Committing the time each week to my drawing practice results in seeds of possibilities that I can then transform into a painting, poem, or leave as is in my drawing pad.

When the meditation is over, before speaking, there is a small window of time when I feel the most free and open to draw. This is when I am the most non-judgmental and non-critical with my markings from scribbles to realistic imagery. I make as many images as I am moved to make from as few as two or three to as many as ten. Just as low light at a dinner table invites intimacy, the silence and low light in the studio provide the right environment for intimate communion for each person with their work. Usually after about fifteen minutes or less of drawing, it feels like a curtain comes down and once again I am back to my *everyday self* and I can tell that the drawing time is over. Once the intellect takes over, the drawings almost always become more contrived and self-conscious. It is the process, not a product or end result that yields the unfolding, the trust, which then allows me to get under my discursive thinking and pull up information and inspiration from the depths of my being where my life experience is truly alive.

Emotional expression is one of the greatest tools we have available to increase our overall sense of wellbeing. Just watch a child dance, sing, draw with crayons or markers, talk to themselves while pretending with their toys, or scream at the top of their lungs at some injustice. Leave them alone for a while and they come back to us in a more balanced place. Children understand the human need to get what's going on *inside* of them *out* into the open. All too often, adults don't give themselves an outlet for emotional expression; or don't avail themselves of it due to years of being criticized—most deeply by themselves. It becomes difficult to get what's deep inside in the dark out into the light. Within our workshop environment, working in silence with charcoal on large smooth paper offers immediate access to emotional release. The visual voice can be loud or soft – both are available in the safety of the silence and trust of those participating with us. There are no demands, and no lessons or tests. Even if someone's intention at the beginning is socially based, eventually deep undercurrents begin shifting within, and they find themselves moving into a totally different "operating system" from when they started. For me, the process of doing the drawing week after week has gotten me to the point where my guard *lets go* and I open my heart and speak the moment I pick up the charcoal.

Eventually, I realized that growth is a cyclical process not linear. Some images are scribbles of emotional content. Some of the drawings invite a greater depth of exploration and those images I will turn into artwork. Wanting a particular kind of imagery doesn't get me there. It is necessary to learn to appreciate the process and let the result take care of itself. In time there is a shift—instead of being short-term result orientated, I have become long term process oriented and grateful when something comes through me as a teaching, a new insight, or an image to explore with paint or write about.

The materials used in the workshop are expendable. Inexpensive paper and soft charcoal give me permission to make the worst looking picture imaginable. In so doing, I get the possibility of receiving the best picture imaginable. When I scream or laugh or cry or find power on paper, the image and the release of the emotion put into the image becomes visible to be looked at over and over again. With enough looking, with enough seeing, understanding comes through. I use only soft black charcoal on large pads of paper. Charcoal is very responsive to the fingers and hand—whispering in the lightest, softest of tones, as well as being capable of putting down very dark strokes that speak loud and clear.

The Light Comes from Within ~ 2012

The movement and quality of the line is affected by using the side or the point of the charcoal. Over time, I have learned the language of the charcoal medium. I create images with black strokes or by leaving the white space of the paper to become the image. When I first started this work, I was such a novice to drawing; I use to say I couldn't draw my way out of a paper bag! All my art training was in photography. It was doing the drawings week after week that taught me how to get on paper what I wanted, or at least close to what I intended. And then it was painting that taught me how to paint.

Using a color medium for drawing such as pastels, would invite analyzing and decision making into the drawing process. Making decisions often causes us to pause, deliberate and question. This interrupts the energy flow. Rather, what I want is to put down on paper what I felt—what I mean to say without judging. By using the simplest tools, I can keep a close connection to my intentions by using large arm movements across the large pad of paper, rubbing, or blurring the blackness of the charcoal with my fingers, or palm of my hand. This keeps the pure energy alive that can be released with emotional directness onto the paper.

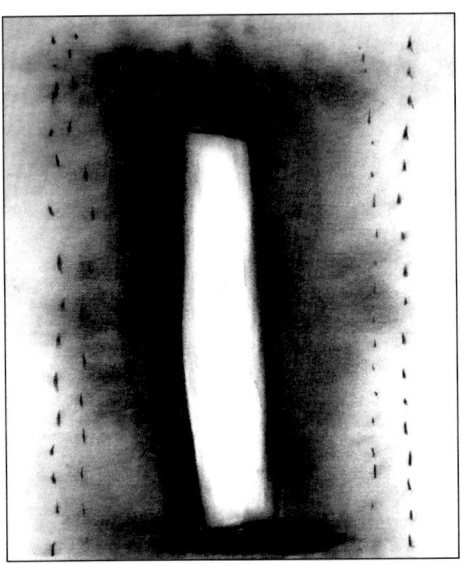

Opening ~ 2014

Sharing

*"Our value is mirrored back to us . . .
only when we share the treasure we already are."*

~ Bryant McGill, Simple Reminders

There's a vortex of energy created when meditating in a group that is unlike the experience of meditating alone. The individual experiences within a group tend to be deeper, and fuller. What completes this process of healing, knowing, and expressing self, is what takes place within the interaction of the group. When it comes time to turn on the small light and gather together to share our stories, we are revealing ourselves to the others. This takes courage; however it is the beginning of self-acceptance which leads to self-love which leads to wholeness in all aspects of our life. The conversations that are generated within the group about our drawings are equally as nourishing as the meditation and drawing aspects. One of the most important qualities we gain with our sharing is that of generosity. Our conversations are positive comments about the drawings as well as conversations that deal with deeper life experiences we each bring to our stories. Generosity of spirit and speaking from the heart gives to each of us a feeling of lightness and joy we take with us into the days ahead until we meet again.

After we finish drawing, one at a time, and still in silence, we get up and sit at a small table and choose a Rune. **The Book of Runes**—*A handbook for the use of an ancient oracle* with commentary by **Ralph Blum**, has been our companion since the beginning and it looks it! The pages are coming loose and some are stained from water damage, but I would never trade it for a new one. Each week, we pick one Rune from the little bag holding 25 stones with symbols on them. Then we read about its meaning in the book. The interpretation never fails to give each of us guidance, and food for thought. On the table is a small pad of paper to copy down a sentence or two that we find particularly compelling that week.

One sentence I never tire of reading is from the Rune of Wholeness: *Sowelu*

"...Seeking after wholeness is the Spiritual Warrior's quest. And yet what you are striving to become in actuality is what you, by nature, already are. You must become conscious of your essence—*your personal myth*—and bring it into form, express it in a creative way."

Just what MedArt is all about!

One evening, about a year ago, I drew a woman with seeds falling from her out-stretched arms. The image told the story of seeds that we all have within us – potential development at various ages. A few months later, another image of a seed appeared, weeks later, another. The story unfolded slowly and for months at a time I didn't give it a thought. However, every now and then, when a *seed woman* image arrived as a charcoal drawing, I'd make some notations of the journey. I liked the story and was inspired to paint a picture of the *seed woman*. The result of my notes, the story, poem and the painting, has been the inspiration for this book.

Seed Woman ~ 2013

Seed Woman

Long, long ago,

back when the world was young

and Mother West Wind's merry little breezes

tumbled and played throughout the hills and valleys,

Seed Woman

opened her arms

and seeds spilled forth into the hearts of each and every child;

seeds of compassion, generosity, and awareness.

When conditions were

just right

and the time was

NOW,

each seed began to crack.

It's thick shell

splitting

open

revealing:

transformation,

regeneration,

new growth,

new self,

in the name of love

Holy love.

Manifestation and Integration

Passage through the dark
into the light
occurs with a
leap of the heart.

Looking back at my paintings, writing, and the career choices I've made since I first began this process, I can see where I struggled and wrestled with opening myself up despite feeling vulnerable and frightened. Throughout it all, I kept thinking of a poem that I wrote back in 1989 titled *One End Open*, and because of a certain internal *knowing*, I took to heart the last lines of the poem and said *"yes"* to offers that were presented to me that I would otherwise have been much too frightened or too insecure to agree to. It is in retrospect that I see what this practice has given me. I see how my intuition has led me through changes and my cycles of growth. I let go of my doubts, my thoughts of not being as qualified as I thought I should be, and all my internal negative voices in general. I finally said YES and rode the waves that brought me through a great deal of fear when trying new things and into so much love and happiness.

One End Open

He took me by the hand and said:

"Sit down, have a cup of tea with me."

Quiet sips of soothing warmth

order . . . tranquility.

No word was spoken,

much was said—

grass mat,

bare floor,

one wall not there.

Hand in hand we stood,

our faces to the breeze;

calm water,

lotus blooms,

wooden walkway,

stones.

Through a white mist he revealed

far, far below me

a city of people

crowded, laughing.

I felt the pull and longing.

I felt my quiet, deep.

I looked at him with sadness:

"How do I make the bridge?"

"The path is in place

just keep walking.

Trusting Self always leaves

One

End

Open."

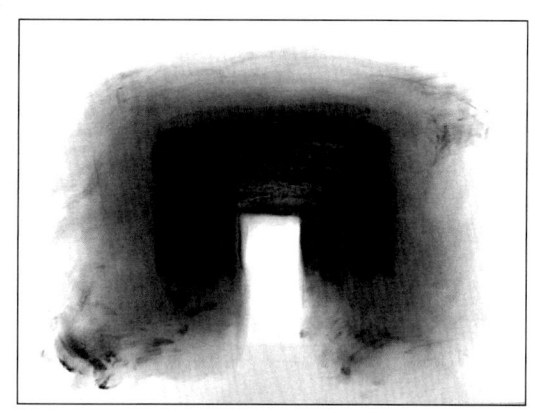

"Remember, the entrance door to the sanctuary is inside you."

~Rumi

Tear in the Veil

Fourteen centuries of tears

I'm crying through fourteen centuries of unshed tears.

Who will help me

I'm all alone.

"Om mani padme hum.

Om mani padme hum.

Om mani padme hum . . ."

and the words come from the end of my pen:

"I can't help you if you tell me its my fault."

"I can help you if you tell me you're afraid."

Who is speaking,

you to me—me to you,

or is it

Self to self?

Cry: a verb,

an action which leads to surrender.

Admit the wound—release the blame,

let go,

cry.

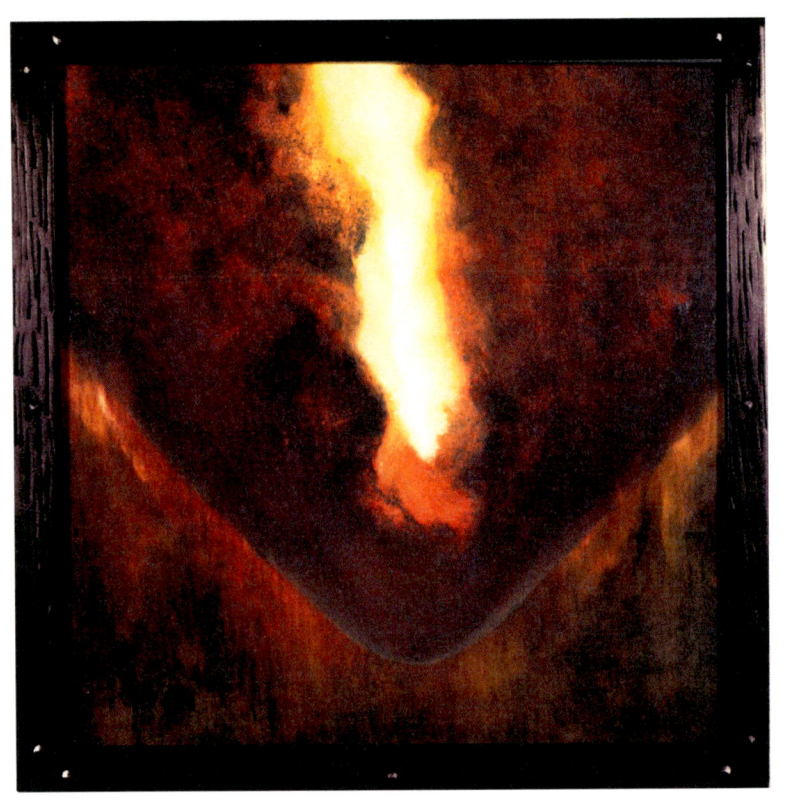

Heart Wound

Be with me

please,

bear me witness

while I bleed . . .

Pain jumps deep into my craw and there is no explanation

no soothing balm which will give comfort.

No person capable of soaking up the pain

with rags to cart away.

The wound exists

and shall exist for as long as it needs to be

raw,

open.

Breaking Through Self Will

I see my will is in the way.
Self will is very strong—
and the belief that I am in control.
I don't dare yield to the invisible support systems
that intuitively I know are there.
I have witnessed them.
They are true, and yet I keep forgetting—
trust has yet to seep down into my core level.
Breaking through self will
can release me
to that knowing place where I am
connected to the universal consciousness—
that which lives and breathes beyond my control,
the place where
no fear exists
and trust abides.
Trusting requires the courage to surrender self will;
yield and allow.
"*Thy* will be done . . ."

Ebony Boy with Gift of Gold

Deep within this meditation I found myself in a dark forest.

Among the shadows, I could see a boy coming toward me

and in his hands was a nugget of gold.

A present for me.

Later, when trying to figure out what could be going on here,
I remembered what I had read of one's shadow.
I had always assumed that the shadow contained memories
and feelings of shame, guilt, rage—those things we keep buried
and don't want others to see.
Then I started to read about this subject in a more directed way and came across:

"if you bring forth what is within you,
what you bring forth will save you.
If you do not bring forth what is within you
what you do not bring forth will destroy you."
—*Gnostic Gospels* by Elaine Pagels words attributed to Jesus in the Gospel of Thomas

About six months after I had completed this painting,
I found the following words in a book by Robert Johnson:

"Jung warned us that it would not be too difficult to get the skeletons
out of the closet from a patient in analysis but it would be
exceedingly difficult to get the gold out of the shadow.
People are as frightened of their capacity
for nobility as of their darkest sides."
—*Owning Your Own Shadow* by Robert Johnson

I keep this painting on my studio wall to remind myself not to let fear hide my gold.

The Gap

As my hand raced back and forth—back and forth—along this incomplete circle,

I realized: "Oh my, this is what I do all the time."

I repeat the familiar, expecting all my dreams to come true.

The open part—the inside and outside of this circle

is where the web of spirit abides.

To get beyond the known,

I have to cross a seemingly empty space.

The unknown—

look up

look in

take the leap.

If I had magic eyes, I could see

all the threads and ladders of support

instead of believing there's only empty space.

Journey of the Pilgrim

With my bag of prayers,

I journey forward—

blood pumping

thick with unknown fear.

Once the path is chosen and

one step taken,

there is no turning back.

I step into the day,

I step into the mystery,

I step into my

Self.

The Two Illusions

Loyal friend and protector

reminds me:

to thine own self be true

and warns

beware of the two illusions:

"I am great!"

"I am worthless."

Harvest

It occurred to me when this image appeared
that I had been holding onto the fruits of my labors long past their ripeness
because of a self imposed concept of perfection and emotional need
to see the whole of the harvest.
My analyzing interrupted the smooth passage from one phase to another.
I passed judgement and
edited out artwork with the slightest hint of a *bruise*
or *broken stem.*

I realize now that
it's the love and energy generated while doing the work then
exchanged with others
that contains the meaning and has a lasting value.
The planting is now.
The growing is now.
The harvest

is

now.

Finding Voice

I pray for guidance and strength to:

Speak who I am.
Trust that I shall be supported
by sources both known and unknown to me now.
Allow my feelings of separateness to dissolve
while allowing my wholeness to come forward and lead the way
even when I don't know how or why.

I have absolutely no idea how my gifts affect others.
The value to them is hidden from me.
Yet, when I speak—revealing
Self through words or paintings,
there is a connection made with another and
I sense the presence of grace.

Prayer Wheel

I knew immediately this was a symbol of life's areas of investigation from the interior to the exterior, but it took painting it to realize what everything meant.

The bottom right hand corner represents the energy of the subconscious self,
such as memories and dreams. This is also the area of the soul which is connected to the greater whole—
the collective unconscious and the river of life.
The soul area is walled off, it takes wanting to gain access.

We have to ask to enter.

Then we have the plains of the mysterious borderland: the connective link between the subconscious and the conscious mind. Big Wyoming fields ready to be plowed and seeded. They are the world of the imagination, and the experiences of meditation. The sparks of insight erupt here first. It is only by cultivating the fields of this borderland that we make pathways, and emotional waterways which connect the soul realm to conscious awareness.

Tending the Soul.

When our fields are well tended and bountiful, we sense a deep connection to man, nature and ultimately God—the source. Around the edge of the wheel are symbols of growth and the rituals that take us into the plains of the borderland. There are symbols of physical reality and symbols of spirit that give us energy through love. Behind the wheel play the musical winds of heaven. This arena beyond the wheel is similar to the inner core except that it represents the heart and soul, which have become illuminated and which we now own so we can give freely of ourselves to others.

Slow Time of the Moon

The light of the moon is an offering
an invitation, if awake,
to illuminate the subtle fields and
dark undercurrents of my life.
It's in the slow time of the moon
I feel most at home.
When nature's poetry comes easily
to the surface
and my life slows to the
attention of
memories, thoughts, revelations
and the awareness of
now.

Woman Who Lives By the Sea

To live a life that reaches
beyond what I know
requires a surrender to that
which comes through me—
opening to that which is within
with grace and gratitude.

Night Bloom

My commitment to a weekly drawing practice isn't about becoming the best charcoal artist or the best oil painter the world has seen. It's about learning to appreciate my own voice—both visual and verbal. It's about learning to be still, to be grateful and comfortable with silence, turn my attention to my interior space and *pay attention* so I can respond to the guidance of my intuition.

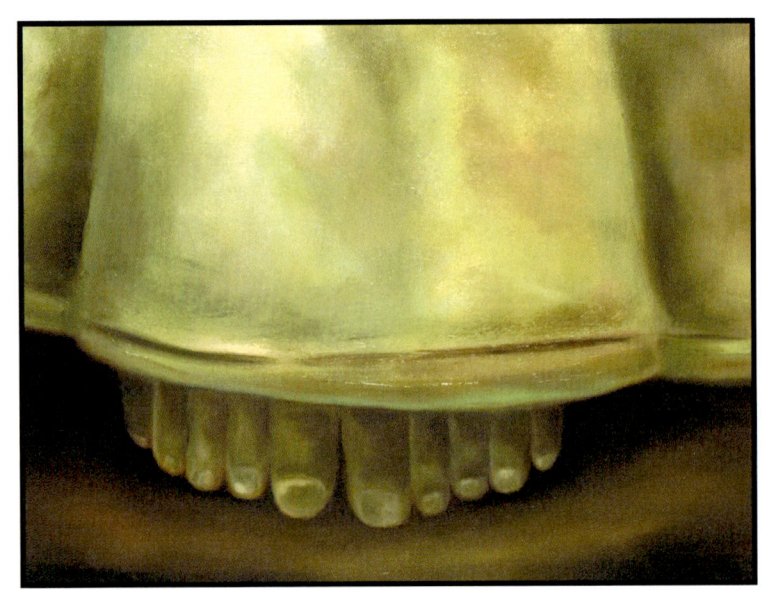

Feet of the Buddha

My observations and what I learned within my drawing practice spilled over into my daily life little by little. At first, I found myself saying *yes* to only that which I wanted to say *yes* to and *no* to the things I really didn't want to do. Then I found myself *asking* for what I wanted with greater confidence.

Before the big real estate boom, our little city had a tannery business. The smell of the hides after being treated with formaldehyde was unbearable. Stacks of the bluish grey hides sat outside the building and we always made sure to roll the windows up in the car if we were driving by. However, by the early 1990's, the tannery was out of business and a local landholder was rehabbing the building into many small units that would later house an incredible bookstore, a little café, a bakery, and several private businesses. I was one of the lucky ones to manage to obtain a small room to use as my studio. It hadn't been updated much but did have a nice big sink. I asked for a reduced price on the monthly rent and received it. Before this, I had been holding my workshop in other spaces including The Pressroom Gallery, Northern Essex Community College and the Newburyport Art Association, and I was thrilled to have my first very own studio in what is now called The Tannery.

During that period my husband was teaching at the School of the Museum of Fine Arts and our four children had graduated from High School, so I was very comfortable being away from home and also very happy to have my own space. It was here at the Tannery that I met Pat Lutz who has a nice large studio space to teach art to adults and children. We met as I sat on the floor of the bookstore next to her studio and we began a conversation. We shared many laughs and good talks about the books we were reading, our paintings, teaching, and life in general. One day when I stopped in to visit her, out of the blue she asked me what I was writing. I had told no one that I had been writing the poetry that accompanied many of my paintings. In fact, I had never written anything before this.
"Why do you ask me that?"
"God asked me to ask you that."
And so began what became my limited edition book of paintings inspired by the charcoal drawings I made in my Drawing Into Creative Wholeness workshop. I called it *One End Open* after the last line of the poem that has guided my decision making since I wrote it in 1992. *(page 22)*

I enjoyed many years of painting and holding my workshops in that space until the rent went up beyond my comfort range. But by then, I *trusted* that something else would come to me. I asked to have the increase gradually increase over three months. That was granted.

During the next three months, my husband Carl and I proceeded to make a studio out of the dilapidated single car garage behind our house. It had a dirt floor and was sinking into the ground on the left side. We had just enough money for a large dumpster so that's where we began. My family was very supportive and Carl, an amazing craftsman, took on the reconstruction work. We emptied out everything that was in the garage: old tires, car parts, and lots of odds and ends that were crammed into that little space over 15 years by us and our four children, especially our three boys. Meanwhile, I sold a large painting, the proceeds from which were enough to cover the building supplies needed to complete the job.

We jacked up the building, replaced the sills, insulated, and hung the sheetrock with the help of friends. My sons helped and were there for us when it came time to install a new roof. A friend had a pair of old exterior french doors and gave them to me to install on the back wall. This really opened up my small space beautifully. I painted and stained inside and out and voila! I was in business. I now had my very own studio and what a treat it is to walk across the driveway and enter my very own space each morning. Even in the winter, it is lovely. It was in this studio that I completed work on *One End Open*. A limited edition of 40 hard bound books with clamshell cases, *One End Open* is a chronicle of my favorite writings and paintings inspired by the meditations and charcoal drawings I'd done over the previous ten years.

I was fortunate to receive a private grant from a woman who had seen my mock-up and wanted a copy of the book. This enabled me to complete the digital printing and afford the hard cover binding and clam shell case with embossed stamp.

Fine quality digital printing was in its infancy back in 1999 so it was quite an achievement. Carl and I worked together to achieve the color I wanted using printers at the School of the Museum of Fine Arts where he was a professor. He was and is my hero of all things digital. Plus, unlike myself, he has a gift for dealing with machines. We produced 40 copies and only a few remain.

The little 12 x 18 foot studio worked for me for many years. I painted, sold paintings, and continued teaching my Drawing Into Creative Wholeness workshops and giving painting lessons to a few adults and children. After several years, I began to want more. I wanted to belong to a bigger community of like-minded souls. I felt that I could do more. I began to silently ask for help in my meditations: *"Please, lead me to a community where I can be one of many working for something greater than myself."* I repeated this prayer every now and then for about two years, and then one day, I received a call from a Montessori school a few towns over.

One very talented child I was teaching in my studio interviewed for admittance to this school and after showing her portfolio to the Head of School he asked her: *"Who's your art teacher?"* He called and asked me to be their school's art specialist. Thus beginning my teaching career. I can't tell you how terrified yet happy I felt when I said *yes* to his offer. This call must be what I had been asking for. For the first year, I went to the ocean's shore every day before I went to school and *let go*. *"There must be a reason I've been asked to be here. I don't have to know why, I just have to show up, do my very best, and learn."* And learn I did. I was the school's Montessori art teacher for twelve years working with about 180 students in first through eighth grade. Each year was a true blessing. I never left the school without a smile on my face. I learned so much about being a leader, listening, and inspiring young artists. I loved coming up with ideas each week for art projects, but most of all, I learned something about the creative thinking process in young children. I also learned that as a teacher, my creative achievements were not important. If I hadn't had the experience of my workshop behind me, I'm not sure I would have recognized this. What came to be the most important part of my teaching was recognizing the importance of the ideas of the children and how my experiences in the art world allowed me to support and encourage them in *their* artistic endeavors. After many years of teaching following a choice-based art approach (Teaching for Artistic Behavior.com), I wrote a book titled *Sticks* (available on Amazon), about the importance of children doing sculptural art and working with their hands in the Lower Elementary grades. By observing children I saw how their craftsmanship grew from three dimensional *scribble* work in the first grade to producing finely controlled identifiable objects by the 4th grade. It was interesting that the student doing scribble work was just as pleased with what they had created as the child who made a recognizable jet plane. The young artist sees the intention put into their work and is not critical or judgemental of the result.

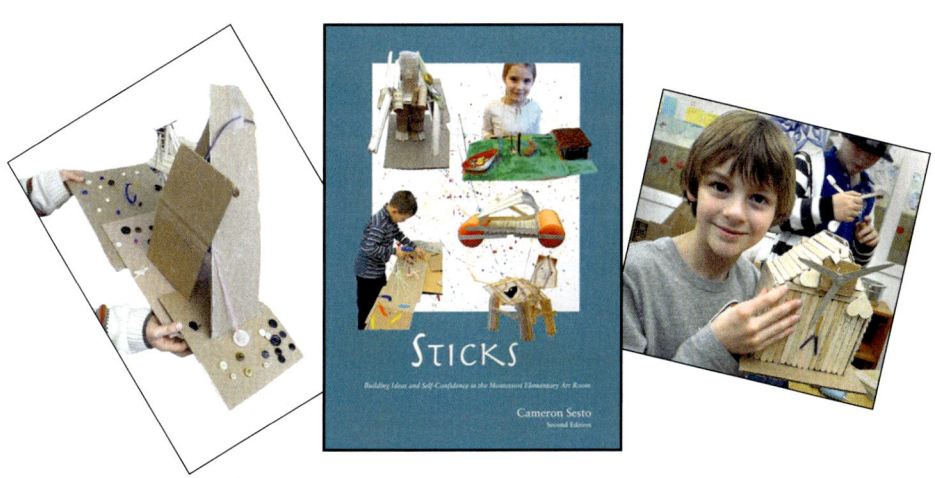

Each year, our art show at the school highlighted many of the inventions the children had created. Like a fifth grader's Avatar inspired by seeing the movie of the same name by James Cameron, dogs on leashes made out of a swim noodle by first graders, or a little creature called "typeface" created from clay and newspaper a middle school student made (above). Each child excitedly told stories about their work as they showed their parents and friends around the displays filled with two and three-dimensional art. My days were filled with laughter, hugs and sad goodbye's at graduation after working with them for their eight years at the school.

One of the pleasures of my 40 minute commute to school, was listing to podcasts. I especially liked listening to interviews by Krista Tippet on her show: *On Being*, and Tami Simon from *Sounds True*. One day while driving to work in 2010, I was listening to an Eckhart Tolle interview and he mentioned something about answering a call. I can't remember exactly what that was all about, but I got chills up and down my arms and I knew it was time for me to move on. I was of retirement age and knew that there was more for me to do outside of teaching art to children. I wanted to continue to teach, but perhaps needed a different venue.

In June 2011, after twelve years, I left my wonderful school and added a 15 x 20 foot addition to my studio. The commitment to this drawing practice each week brings about a centering within me that brings me peace, courage and trust, teaching me that creativity moves *through* me, and is not *of* me. I wanted to increase public awareness of my workshop and have more people share the experience that has so enriched my life for almost thirty years. When we are in school we add knowledge to our thinking minds and we can reason better. When we go within, we add wisdom to our heart mind. The heart mind is where intuition and feelings are located. These are the main ingredients for self-guidance, empathy, and compassion.

Understanding the cycles of my own creativity has led me to trust myself to step out of my comfort zone and bring my voice confidently into my community in spite of the inevitable remnants of fear. For fear never really leaves us if we try something new every now and then. To me, a little bit of fear and anxiety tell me that I'm growing. What is just right for me today might feel like a tight shoe tomorrow, and I'll be pushing into yet another cycle of being. What the future holds is an unknown filled with possibility. What I do know for sure is that trusting my intuition has always brought me into a place of growth, and if not immediate, eventual happiness. Learning how to "tune in" and listen to my intuition using meditation and visual expression has been my greatest teacher.

I recently purchased Carl Jung's *Red Book* and found this passage to be so relevant to my work:

"The year 1913 was pivotal in Jung's life. He began a self-experiment that became known as his "confrontation with the unconscious" and it lasted until 1930. During this experiment, he developed a technique to "get to the bottom of (his) inner processes," "to translate the emotions into images," and "to grasp the fantasies which were stirring underground." He later called this method "active imagination." He first recorded these fantasies in his *Black Books*. He then revised these texts, added his commentary, and copied them using a calligraphic script into a book entitled *Liber Novus* bound in red leather and accompanied by his own paintings.

"The years, of which I have spoken to you, when I pursued the inner images, were the most important time of my life. Everything else is to be derived from this. It began at that time, and the later details hardly matter anymore. My entire life consisted in elaborating what had burst forth from the unconscious land flooded me like an enigmatic stream and threatened to break me. That was the stuff and material for more than only one life. Everything later was merely the outer classification, the scientific elaboration, and the integration into life. But the numinous beginning which contained everything was then." C.G. Jung

I can say the same thing about **Drawing into Creative Wholeness** then and now.

The Notebook ~ 2011

The following are quotes are from three participants who have been committed to and have shared this process with me for many years:

"MedArt—it's a calling of souls to journey, journey inward. It's an exploration of truths, our personal and universal truths. A time set aside for moving deeper into the meaning of my life and the meaning of life on this planet. The combination of sacred space, meditation, drawing, and choosing a rune at the end of the evening, gives me ample opportunity to receive a universal message every week!

These messages stay with me all week. I often use my message in my teaching and yoga classes for that week. The quotes often resonate with my students. In fact, a quote from the rune "The Self, Mannaz" says it all "Strive to live the ordinary life in a non-ordinary way." That's what MedArt offers me. ~Rose Russo, yoga instructor RYT-200, artist, designer

"The art and meditation group, coupled with Cameron's wise and kind leadership, have become a wonderful addition to my life. Experiencing community, quiet meditation, and safe space has encouraged me to creatively explore inner and outer landscapes. These experiences have been revealing, restorative and fun!"
~Anne Mulvey Ph.D, creative writer, InterPlay leader, professor emerita, UMass Lowell

"I was originally drawn to MedArt by Cameron's beautiful and soulful paintings. They touched such a deep place in me. I was lucky to get a spot in her class 15 years ago and began studying with her.
Eventually I moved and drifted away from MedArt. Some years went by and then, during a very challenging time in my life, I had a dream: Like a bird, I was flying over Newbury, seeing so much ordinary life going on in the small community. My attention was captured by a house with a building behind it where people were gathered. A voice in my dream said: *"Something REAL is going on here."* I knew the house was Cameron's, but the building was not familiar to me; it was much larger than the small studio that I remembered. Since I take my dreams seriously, I contacted her to see if she was still teaching and she welcomed me graciously to her ongoing class. Within the following year, a larger building (the one I saw in my dream) was constructed behind the little studio, becoming the main place of meetings, meditation, and drawing together. What a gift in my life to be loved into being through this gentle and nourishing process! ~Alison Davis, artist, poet, designer.

Cameron Sesto

"Working with this method since 1986 has shown me the cycles of creativity, how to work within them, and taught me so much about the personal and the universal personal experiences we all share."

A retired Montessori art teacher, Cameron currently facilitates meditation and visual expression workshops, and is the founder and director of the *Center for Creative Wholeness*. She lives with her husband on the North Shore of Massachusetts in the home near the ocean where they raised their four children and now welcome their nine grandchildren. Cameron holds a Photography degree from the Rochester Institute of Technology and is a self-taught oil painter, sculptor and designer. She has written, illustrated, and designed four books of her artwork and her work with children including **Sticks**, and **Simply Great**.

Drawing into Creative Wholeness, 2014 —More copies of this book are available on **Amazon.com**

Sticks, 2008—building ideas and self-confidence in the Montessori Lower Elementary art room. Cameron's observations reveal how biology and psychology meet and are strengthened through the artistic behavior of children ages 6 to 9. **Sticks** is illustrated with full color photographs by the author. **Available on Amazon.com**

Wisdom Bowls, 2002—by Meredith Young-Sowers, with introduction by Caroline Myss. **Interior Art by Cameron Sesto,** published by Stillpoint Publishing, New Hampshire

One End Open, 1999—a compilation of prose, poetry, and paintings originating from her workshop: *Drawing into Creative Wholeness* that combines meditation and visual expression. Limited Edition of 40 books hardbound in a clamshell case. Only 5 remain.
Reviewed: Holistic Times October, 2000

Simply Great, 1989—a cooking instruction manual for teachers of non-readers Cameron developed while teaching the intellectually disabled workers at Opportunity Works in Newburyport, MA. published by MDC University of Wisconsin and the Center for Independent Living. **Reviewed:** Boston Globe October, 1990

Information about Cameron's workshops and artwork can be seen on her web sites: **cameronart.com** and at **centerforcreativewholeness.com**

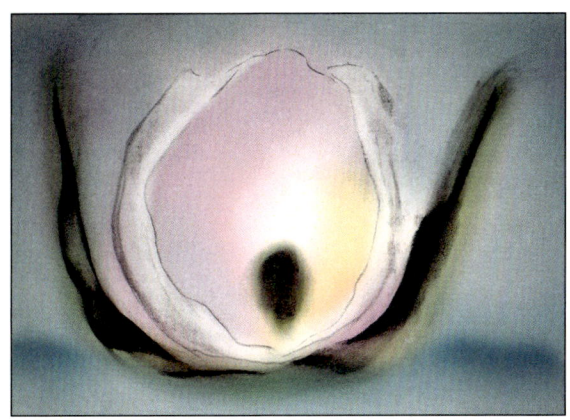

Go Deep and Bloom ~ 2014

"Your vision will become clear only when you can look into your own heart. Who looks outside, dreams, who looks inside, awakens."

Carl Jung

centerforcreativewholeness.com

"When I know who I am,

When I value who I am,

When I trust who I am,

I can give freely to others

All that I am—

And my journey into wholeness

will have begun."

Excerpt from creative wholeness meditation by Cameron Sesto

Made in the USA
San Bernardino, CA
08 March 2018